Feathers, Fins, and Fur

I love giraffes and jellyfish,
leopards, and long-eared hares,
and guppies, puppies, loons, baboons,
penguins, and polar bears.

I love wombats and walruses,
and things that grrr! and purr,
and all the creatures God has made
with feathers, fins, and fur.

~ Eileen Berry

Reading *1B* for Christian Schools™ | Third Edition

BJU PRESS
GREENVILLE, SOUTH CAROLINA

READING 1B for Christian Schools™
Feathers, Fins, and Fur
Third Edition

Coordinating Authors	**Designers**	**Composition**
Susan J. Lehman	Holly Gilbert	Carol Larson
Linda O. Parker	David Siglin	

Editor	**Cover**	**Photo Acquisition**
Debbie L. Parker	Elly Kalagayan	Joyce Landis
		Carla Thomas

Project Manager
Victor Ludlum

Acknowledgments
"Cat Kisses" by Bobbi Katz, Copyright © 1974. Renewed 1996 by Bobbi Katz. Reprinted with permission of the author.

Photo credits are listed on page 92.

for Christian Schools is a registered trademark of BJU Press.

ISBN 1-59166-268-0

15   14   13   12   11   10   9   8   7   6   5   4   3   2

Contents

Feathers, Fins, and Fur

Grandma's Kisses

L. Michelle Rosier
illustrated by Keith Neely

The Pictures

"Grandma! Grandma!"
Marta ran to Grandma.
Marta set a red bag on the deck.
Grandma had a kiss for Marta.

1

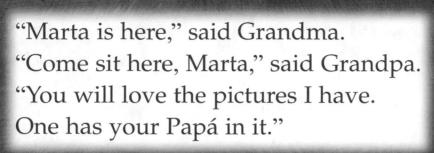

"Marta is here," said Grandma.
"Come sit here, Marta," said Grandpa.
"You will love the pictures I have.
One has your Papá in it."

2

"Here is your Papá and his dog.
Tuff was a brown and white dog.
Tuff ran fast in the sand."

"Here is Bess," said Grandpa.
"Bess was a big black cat.
Bess sat in the sun."

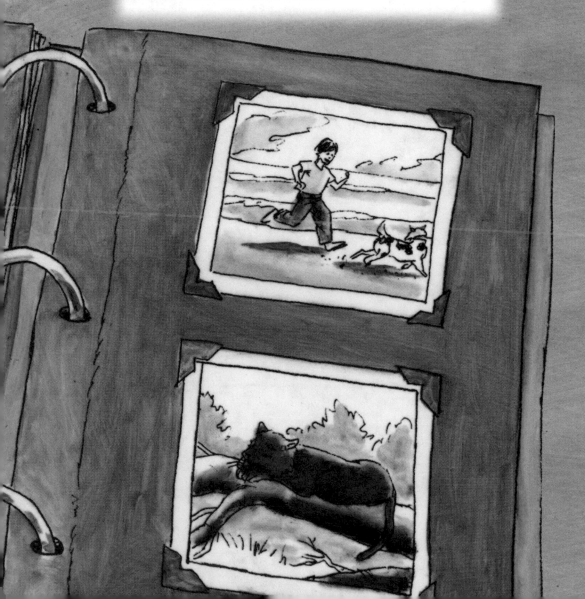

"This picture has lots of pigs.
Pigs love the mud," said Grandma.
"Grandpa fed the pigs."

"And here are the hens.
I had ten hens.
I got many eggs."

4

Pretty Loro

"I love the dogs and cats.
I love the pigs and hens.
But I love your parrot best.
Tell of pretty Loro," said Marta.

5

"Pretty Loro, yellow and blue,
Can peck and give a kiss to you.
Pretty Loro, green and red.
'Pretty parrot,' Loro said."

"Off to bed," Grandma said.

Grandma tells God, "I love You."
Marta tells God, "I love You."

7

Grandma gets a big hug.
Marta gets kisses.

Grandma sits and rocks.
Marta and Loro sleep.

8

A Talking Parrot

Draw a line from each word to complete each phrase.

Marta

Loro

Papa

Grandma

is yellow, blue, green, and red.

sleeps in a bed.

sits and rocks.

had a brown and white dog.

A Pet for Clem

Becky Davis
illustrated by Tim Davis

What Pet?

"Clem," said Mom, "Dad and I want to get a pet for you."

"What pet do you want?" said Dad.

Clem sat and sat.
Clem did not want a cat.
Clem did not want a dog.
Clem did not want a duck.
And Clem did not want a white rat.

At last Clem said, "I want a yak."

"A yak?" said Dad.

"Yes, a yak," said Clem.
"I want a big, black yak.
I do not want any other pet.
I want the blackest yak yet."

The Best Pet

"If I had a yak,
I would hop on his back
and do flip-flops on top," Clem said.
"And the yak and I would clip-clop
up the block."

"And I could click a clacker
and flick a flag.
And you and Mom could clap for us."

"Well, Clem," said Dad. "Mom and I went
to get a pet for you.
And I said to the man,
'A dog can flip,
and a cat can flop.
But they are not what Clem would want.'

'And a hen can cluck,
and a duck can flap.
But they are not what Clem would want.'

And Mom said, 'Clem would want a yak.
Clem would want a big, plump, black yak.'"

"And a yak is what Mom and I got for
you," said Dad.
"Here it is, Clem.
Hop on the back
of your big, black yak!"

The Lion and the Elk

a fable adapted by Gail Fitzgerald
illustrated by Del Thompson

A lion got up from his nap.
"I am hungry," the lion said.
And the lion crept to a pond.
A rabbit slept at the pond.

18

Just as the lion got to the rabbit,
a big elk ran past.
"I am hungry," the lion said to himself.
"An elk is big.
A rabbit is not as big as an elk."
And the lion let the rabbit run away.

The elk was big.
But the elk was fast.
And the elk got away.

The lion crept back to get the rabbit.
But the rabbit was not at the pond.
"The elk ran away, and the rabbit ran away," the lion said.
"And I am still hungry."

Moral: A bird in the hand is worth two in the bush.

A Snack for Two

Kathleen Hynicka

illustrated by Kathy Pflug

The Wish

Fran got a blue dish from the top shelf.
Fran got a glass from the top shelf.
Fran got crackers and jam from the next shelf.
Fran was sad.
"A snack for one just will not do.
I wish I could have a snack for
two," said Fran.

22

"One dish will not do for a snack for two.
And one glass will not do," Fran said.

One blue dish went back on the top shelf.
One blue glass went back on the top shelf.
The crackers and jam went back on the
next shelf.

Fran sat on a stump.
"I have a big wish," the fox said.

Not One but Two

Grass was swishing.
Twigs went crack.

"Who is it?" said Fran.
Bess ran to the den.
Bess held up a bag.
"Here are boxes for you," Bess said.
"Not one but two.
They are gifts from Mother Fox."

25

Fran lifted the lid from one box.
Mother Fox had put a pretty blue dish
in the box.
The other box had a blue glass.

"Just what I wanted!" said Fran.
"I have two dishes.
I have two glasses.
Will you have a snack?"
said Fran.

Fran put two blue dishes on the log.
Fran put two glasses on the log.

"I have a box of crackers," Fran said.
"Will plum jam do?"

"Yes, plum jam will do," said Bess.
"I love crackers and jam.
It is a snack for two."

Fran's Plan

Fill in the bubble of the word that matches the picture.

 ● dish   ○ dash   ○ drum

 ○ grub   ○ give   ● glass

 ● gift   ○ grass   ○ gum

 ○ cub   ○ crib   ● crackers

 ○ stick   ● stump   ○ stop

John's Creatures

A biography of John Audubon
retold by Karen Wilt

The Nest

"John, what is in your lunch bucket?"

"It is the nest of a finch, Mother.
It has eggshells in it," John said.

"But where is the finch?" his mother said.

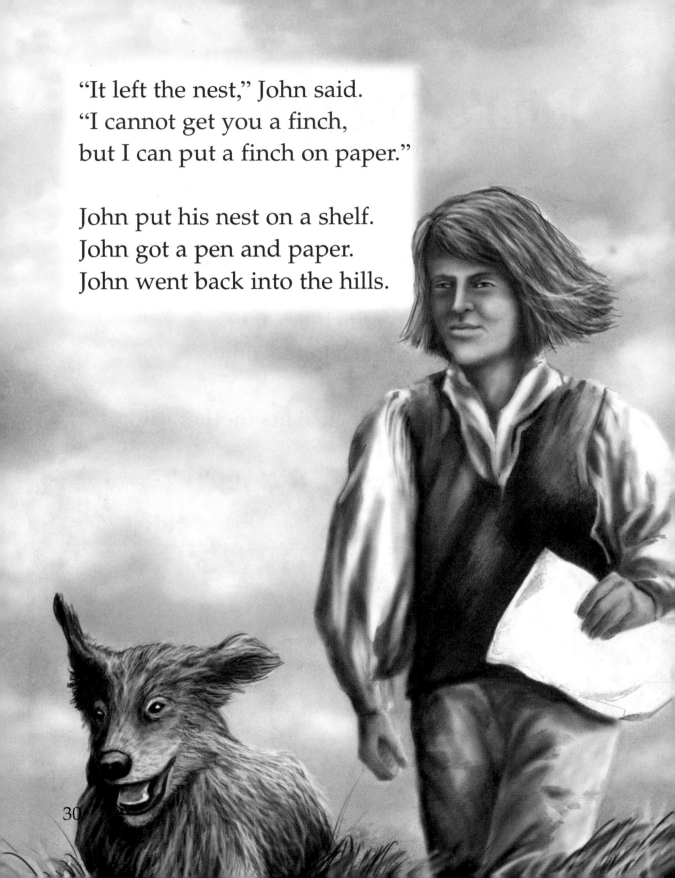

"It left the nest," John said.
"I cannot get you a finch,
but I can put a finch on paper."

John put his nest on a shelf.
John got a pen and paper.
John went back into the hills.

John was still.
A finch sat on a branch.
John put the finch on paper.
Here is what John did.

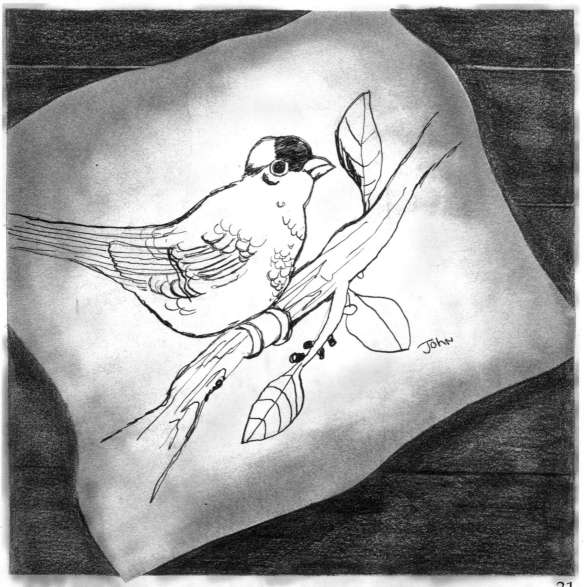

John's Paintings

John's finch did not have any color.
John wanted to paint the finch.
And John did.

John got some watercolors and a brush.
John painted a hummingbird on a red bud.
John painted a blue jay on a branch.
John painted a robin as it sang.

John hung some of his paintings.
And John put some in a box.
John put the box under his bed.
Rats got into his paintings.

John could not fix the paintings.
John had to do other paintings.
John did not give up.
And his paintings got better and better.
Here is one of John's paintings.

Seek and Find

Circle the correct answer.

1. What was in the lunch bucket?

2. What did John take to the hills?

3. Where did John put the box of paintings?

A Bed for Buddy

Dottie Oberholzer
illustrated by Keith Neely

The Bed

Dad sits at his big brown desk.
Buddy wants a nap.
Dad said, "Buddy, nap there on the rug
in the sun."
But Buddy gets under Dad's desk
and naps there.

Ashley is hanging up some pictures.
Buddy gets under Ashley's bed
and naps there.

Mom is dusting a shelf.
Buddy gets under Mom's dresses
and naps there.

39

Alex is doing his music.
Buddy gets under the bench
and naps there.

Buddy must have a bed!
Dad gets a box.
Mom gets a blue and green blanket.
Dad and Mom will fix a bed for Buddy.

"Here it is," said Dad.
"Buddy can have his naps here.
It is a bed just for Buddy."

The Pup Tent

"Get in the bed, Buddy.
It is a pet bed," said Dad.
"It is just for you," said Alex.

Buddy gets into the bed.
But the bed will not do.
Buddy will not nap here.

43

Dad is back at his big brown desk.
Buddy gets the blue and green blanket
from his box.
Buddy puts the blanket under the desk,
and Buddy naps there.

Ashley cannot rest.
Ashley hears Buddy's bell.
The blanket is under the bed,
and Buddy naps there.

45

Mom gets a red dress.
The blanket is under the
dresses, and Buddy naps there.

Alex wants to get to his music.
The blanket is under the bench,
and Buddy naps there.

46

"I get it," said Alex.
"Buddy must have a pup tent!
Let's fix the box for him."
Ashley gets a big red rag.
Alex puts a red top on Buddy's box.

47

"Here it is," said Alex.
"This is the best bed for Buddy."
Buddy gets into the bed.
And Buddy naps there.

Where Does Buddy Nap?

Fill in the bubble next to the correct answer.

Buddy naps under dad's
- ○ rug   ● desk

Buddy naps under mom's
- ● dresses   ○ cup

Buddy naps under Alex's
- ○ bus   ● bench

Buddy naps under Ashley's
- ● bed   ○ tub

Who Are You?

Jan Joss
illustrated by Paula Cheedle

A White Kitten

"Who are you?
You are white.
You can lick.
You have whiskers!"
Josh lifted up the sad kitten.
"When did you come here?" Josh said.

"You are not Matt's cat.
Matt has a white dog.
And you are not Ann's cat.
Ann's cat has yellow eyes.
Your eyes are blue.
Who are you?"

"Here is a kitten, Mom," Josh said.
"It is white, and it has black whiskers.
It is not Ann's cat.
Ann's cat has yellow eyes."
"Bring the kitten," Mom said.
"Let us ask the Greens."

Is It Yours?

Josh and Mom went next door.
Josh rang the bell.
"Is this your kitten?" said Josh.
"This is not Fluff," Ben said.
"Fluff is the biggest cat on the block."

"Here comes Mr. Rush," said Mom.
"You can ask him."
Josh ran to Mr. Rush.
"This kitten got away from its mother,"
Josh said.
"And its mother is not here."

"Mr. Benner's cat has kittens," said
Mr. Rush.
"I will ask him when I give him this
letter."
"And you can ask Mrs. Smith," Mom said.
"I think Mrs. Smith has a cat."
"Yes," Mr. Rush said. "And it has a litter
of kittens."

In the Shed

Mom and Josh rang Mrs. Smith's bell.

"Is this your kitten?" Josh said.

"Yes," Mrs. Smith said.

"I was just thinking of this kitten.
Come to the shed, Josh."

Mrs. Smith's big black cat was napping
on the floor.

"Here are two other kittens," said Josh.

Mrs. Smith bent to pet the white kitten.
"I have a litter of kittens.
That white kitten can drink from a dish.
It can run and jump with you.
You can have the white kitten, Josh."

"Yes, Josh," Mom said.
"The white kitten is yours."
"Thank you, Mrs. Smith," Josh said.
"And thank you, Mom."
Josh lifted the kitten.
"Your eyes are blue.
You are Blue Eyes.
That's who you are!"

Cat Kisses

Bobbi Katz
illustrated by Paula Cheadle

Sandpaper kisses
on a cheek or a chin—
that is the way
for a day to begin!

Sandpaper kisses—
a cuddle, a purr.
I have an alarm clock
that's covered with fur.

A Man and a Bug

Gail Fitzgerald
Based on a true story
illustrated by Stephanie True and Preston Gravely Jr.

A Big Job

The people of Chad do not have Bibles.
Will God send a man there to tell of Jesus?

A man handed Mr. Skinner a box.
Mr. Skinner lifted the box onto the Piper
Cub.

"You have lots of boxes," the man said.
"Will they fit in the Piper Cub?"
"They have to fit," said Mr. Skinner.
"In some boxes are quilts and pots and pans.
And in other boxes are Bibles.

I want to help the people in Chad.
I want to tell the people of Jesus."
The man said, "You have a big job.
Some of the people in Chad will not want
you to tell others of Jesus.
They will want to stop you.
They could kill you.
I will ask God to help you."

63

God Helps

The man did ask God to help Mr. Skinner.
Once the man went to bed but could not rest.
The man got up and sat on his bed.
"Mr. Skinner must have help," the man said
to God.

Away in Chad, Mr. Skinner was landing
his Piper Cub.
Bad men hid on a cliff.
One man shot at the Piper Cub.
But just as the gun went off,
a big bug bit Mr. Skinner on the leg.
Mr. Skinner bent to brush off the bug.
The bullet went into the Piper Cub!

But the bullet went past Mr. Skinner.
The Piper Cub did not crash.

God sent the bug to help Mr. Skinner.
Mr. Skinner got the Bibles to the people.
Mr. Skinner did tell the people of Jesus.
And many people trusted in Jesus.

Go ye therefore, and teach all nations. —Matthew 28:19

Trusting God

Color the bubble to show what happened first.

1. ○ A man handed Mr. Skinner a box.
   ○ A big bug bit Mr. Skinner on the leg.

2. ○ Mr. Skinner got the Bibles to the people.
   ○ The bullet went into the Piper Cub.

Color the Piper Cub.

Money from a Fish

Taken from Matthew 17:24-27
retold by Becky Davis

The Temple Tax

Peter was a fisherman.
But Jesus said, "Come with us."
Peter went with Jesus and did what Jesus said.
The man from the temple said,
"Peter, does your Master give his tax money to the temple?"

And Peter said, "Yes, Jesus does give his tax money to the temple."

Then Peter went to Jesus.

"The man wants the temple tax," Peter said. "But you and I do not have money for the tax."

Jesus said to him, "Peter, get
your fishing string.
Put your little ship in the water.
You will get a single little fish.
It will have money in it.
Get that money.
It is the money for the temple tax.
Give it to the temple man for us."

Fishing

Peter got his fishing string.
Then Peter got on his little ship.
Peter let his ship drift to the middle of
the water.

Peter put a bug on the end of the string.
Then Peter let his string dangle in the water.
Tug! Peter felt a fish grab the bug.
Peter got the fish into the ship.

There was money in the fish, just as Jesus had said.

Peter got the money and went back to the land.

Peter ran to the temple.

Peter and Jesus were glad to give the tax money to the man.

But my God shall supply all your needs. —Philippians 4:19

Fishing for Money

Complete each sentence.

Peter was a _____.
    ● fisherman   ○ camper

Peter got the _____ into the ship.
    ○ kitten   ● fish

Draw the fish that Peter caught.	Draw what Peter found in the fish.
	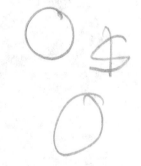

In God's Waters

Ellen Goodwin
illustrated by Kathy Pflug

Some of God's fish are as big as trucks,

but others are as little as pins.

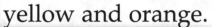

Some fish are drab green and black.
Others are pink and blue and purple and
yellow and orange.

The catfish is not the biggest fish,
but it has a big job.
It snacks on trash and junk.
The catfish is not a trash man.
The catfish is a trash fish.

The flatfish has two eyes, just as
you and I have two eyes.
But its eyes are on top.
Big fish cannot slip up on the flatfish.

If the puffer fish gets upset, it gulps water.

It swells up bigger and bigger and bigger.

Then its prickers stick up on end.

Many fish live in God's waters.
Can you think of any others?

And God said, Let the waters bring forth
abundantly the moving creature that hath life.
—Genesis 1:20

The Silver Thing

Chuck and Jan Joss
illustrated by Holly Hannon

Such a Fuss

Away off in Grassland the insects are upset.
A silver thing flashes in the sun.

The insects put the silver thing on a stump.
One bug stepped up.
"What is this?" said Stinger.
"What can one do with this silver thing?"

81

Mrs. Grasshopper stepped up.
"Such a fuss!" the grasshopper said.
"It is a silver dipper."
But the silver thing did not dip any water.
It dripped on Mrs. Grasshopper.
The silver thing went back on the stump.
THUMP!

"What other job could the silver thing do?"
said Stinger.
The insects stopped to think and think.
"The silver thing must do
something," they said.

A Grand Plan

The insects were still thinking.
"What is this?" said Stinger.
"What can one do with this silver thing?"
The bugs bent to inspect the thing.

Stan Stinkbug grabbed the thing.
"Once I had such a thing," Stan said.
"And I heard pretty music with it."
But it did not send pretty music.
The silver thing went back
on the stump.
THUMP!
THUMP!

Here comes the King.
The King of Grassland will think of a plan.
"A man left this here," said the King.
"It was once a lid for a can.
But it will be something better!"

"Bring some cobwebs," said the King.
"Hang the silver thing from this twig.
The school in Grassland will have a swing.
Little bugs love to swing.
This is what one can do with
the silver thing."

Away off in Grassland the insects
are content.
A silver swing flashes up and back
in the sun.

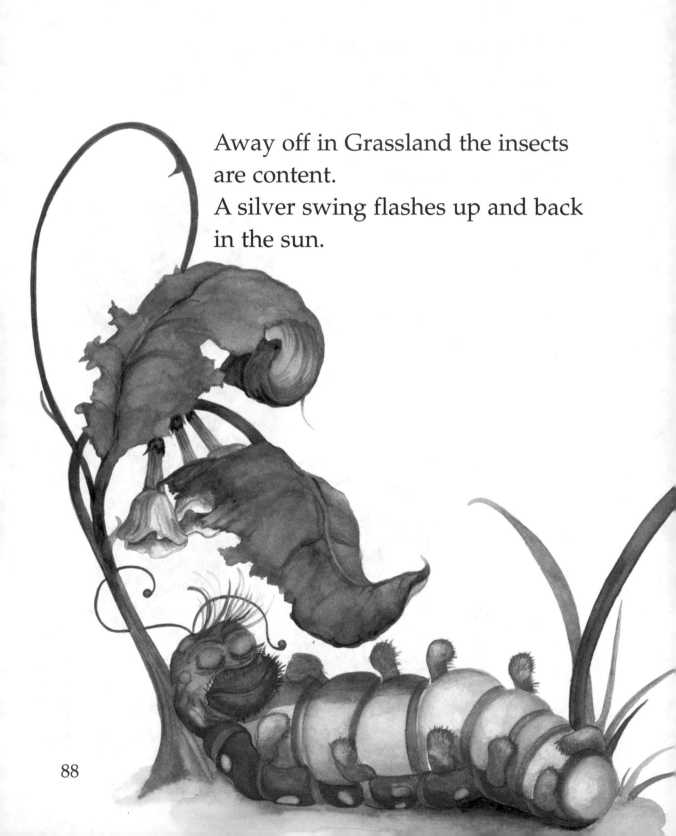

Something Silver

Fill in the bubble next to the correct answer.

What flashes in the sun at Grassland?

○ a bug   ● a thing

Where do the insects put the thing?

○ in a can   ● on a stump

What do little bugs like to do?

● swing   ○ run

What does the silver thing do
to Mrs. Grasshopper?

● drips on her   ○ falls on her

What Is It?

Milly Howard

What is buzzing
and pestering
and stinging Jill?

What is packing
and sticking stuff
away in a nest?

What is winging
and flickering away
in the blue dusk?

What is quacking
and splashing
as it swims
in the pond?

What is pecking
and clucking
as it hunts
in the sand?

What is frisking
and bucking
as it runs
from the man?

Photo Credits

The following agencies and individuals have furnished materials to meet the photographic needs of this textbook. We wish to express our gratitude to them for their important contribution.

Dean E. Biggins
COREL Corporation
Brenda Hansen
Hemera Technologies
James C. Leupold
Dave Menke

National Audubon Society, Inc.
PhotoDisc, Inc.
Schreiner Farms
Carla Thomas
U.S. Fish and Wildlife Service
www.arttoday.com

John's Creatures

Courtesy National Audubon Society, Inc. 35

Glossary

© 2004 Hemera Technologies, Inc. All rights reserved. 93 (bench, cliff), 94 (elk); © 2004 www.arttoday.com 93 (buck), 94 (drip); U.S. Fish and Wildlife Service/photo by Dave Menke 94 (finch); COREL Corporation 94 (dolphins); U.S. Fish and Wildlife Service/photo by James C. Leupold 95 (grasshopper); U.S. Fish and Wildlife Service/photo by Dean E. Biggins 95 (hummingbird); PhotoDisc, Inc. 95 (kitten), 96 (lion, kittens, child napping), 97 (parrot, rabbit); Carla Thomas 97 (quilt); Brenda Hansen 98 (bookshelf); Schreiner Farms 100 (yak)

Glossary

A

a·way

The dog ran away.

B

bench

Sam sat on the bench.

blan·ket

A blanket covers the sleeping baby.

buck

A scared horse can buck its rider off.

C

cliff

The steep cliff hangs over the water.

crack

Dropping the mirror put a crack in it.

D

dip·per

Sally drank water from the dipper.

drip

Water can drip from the faucet.

E

elk

Mr. Custer hunts deer and elk.

F

finch

The finch is making a nest in the tree.

flip

The dolphins like to flip in the water.

G

grass·hop·per

The grasshopper jumps from leaf to leaf.

H

hum·ming·bird

The tiny hummingbird flaps its wings.

I

in·spect

After I clean my room, Mom will inspect it.

J

junk

Grandpa hauled the junk to the dump.

K

kit·ten

The fuzzy kitten drinks from a saucer.

L

lick

I will lick my ice cream cone.

li·on

The lion is the biggest cat in the zoo.

lit·ter

The cat has a litter of five kittens.

M

N

nap

The child will go to bed and nap after lunch.

O

P

paint
The man will paint the walls blue.

par·rot
The green parrot has a cracker
in its bill.

pet
My pet is a rabbit.

pic·ture
Brad hung the picture on the wall.

prick·ers
The prickers on the bush poked
my hand.

Q

quilt
Grandma's quilt covers the bed.

R

rob·in

The red-breasted robin sat on the branch.

S

shed

Dad puts his tools in the shed.

shelf

The books are on the shelf.

T

tem·ple

Men worship God at the temple.

twig

One leaf hangs on the tiny twig.

U

un•der

The snail hid under the rock.

V

W

wa•ter•col•ors

We painted with our watercolors.

whisk•ers

Milk dripped from the cat's whiskers.

X

Y

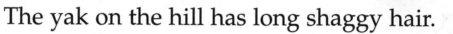

yak

The yak on the hill has long shaggy hair.

Z